The Nature and Science of
BUBBLES

Jane Burton and Kim Taylor

W

FRANKLIN WATTS
NEW YORK • LONDON • SYDNEY

First published in 1998

Franklin Watts
96 Leonard Street
London EC2A 4RH

Franklin Watts Australia
14 Mars Road
Lane Cove
NSW 2066

Conceived, designed and produced by
White Cottage Children's Books
29 Lancaster Park
Richmond, Surrey TW10 6AB, England

Editor/Art Director: Treld Pelkey Bicknell

Educational Consultant: Jane Weaver

Scientific Advisor: Dr Jan Taylor

Set in Rockwell Light by R & B Creative Services

Originated by R & B Creative Services

Printed in Belgium

ISBN: 0 7496 2953 3

Dewey Decimal Classification Number: 532

A CIP catalogue record for this book is available
from the British Library

Contents

Why are Bubbles Round?

Bubbles form when a gas is released into a liquid. Usually the gas is **air** and the liquid is water. But bubbles of other gases such as **oxygen** form in water and you can have gas bubbles in red-hot molten metal, in molten glass or even in treacle.

When an underwater bubble floats to the surface, it does one of two things: it either bursts and disappears altogether or it forms a floating bubble. A floating bubble is quite different from a bubble under the surface because it not only has gas inside but also *outside.* It consists of just a thin **film** of liquid.

Bubbles tend to be round except when they are in contact with each other or with something solid. Then they can have flat surfaces. The reason for the roundness of bubbles is that they are pulled into shape by a force called **surface tension**. Surface tension acts like an invisible **elastic** skin on the surface of all liquids. A bubble floating in the air has both an inside and an outside surface and so there are two lots of surface tension pulling it into a round shape.

The biggest of these bubbles of oxygen are being pushed towards the surface by the **pressure** of the water, but they are held by the green weed that has produced them. Instead of being round, they are pear-shaped.

Floating bubbles are attracted to solid objects and to each other. When they touch something, bubbles can have flat sides, like these bubbles resting against the glass of an aquarium.

Bubbles in Water

Oxygen bubble produced underwater by green water weed. ▲

Green plants in sunlight give off oxygen gas. When water plants do this, the gas forms bubbles. You can sometimes see strings of little oxygen bubbles rising slowly from the stems or leaves of water weed in a pond or aquarium. Bigger bubbles rise more quickly. Large bubbles of **methane** sometimes come rushing to the surface of ponds. Methane, or marsh gas, forms under water when dead plant material rots.

Small bubbles are perfectly round. They are held in shape by surface tension. But surface tension is not strong enough to hold bigger bubbles in shape. Big bubbles become flattened or turned into mushroom shapes and may even break up into smaller bubbles as they wobble up to the surface.

Underwater bubbles trapped beneath ice press against its underside, becoming button-shaped. These methane bubbles rose to the surface at intervals as the lake was freezing. During the time between one bubble rising and the next, the ice thickened, causing columns of bubbles to form inside the ice. ▶

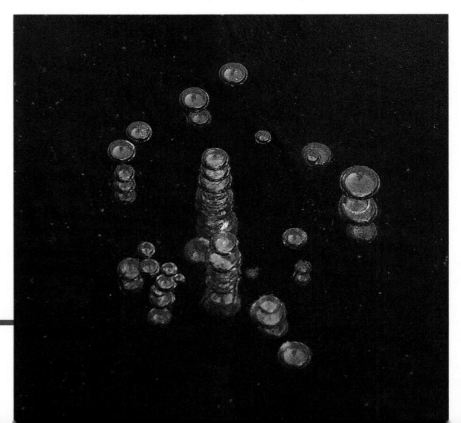

◄

Mud at the bottom of a lake often contains trapped methane gas. The slightest disturbance will cause the gas to bubble up to the surface. As this Avocet walks delicately through the shallow water, it leaves behind a trail of methane bubbles.

The size of a bubble in water depends on pressure. The greater the pressure, the smaller the bubble. Pressure increases the deeper you go, and, at the bottom of the sea there is huge, crushing pressure due to the weight of water up above. Here, a lot of gas is squeezed into a very little space. A bubble the size of a pea in the ocean depths would swell to the size of a football by the time it reached the surface—if it did not break up into thousands of smaller bubbles on the way.

The small bubbles ▲ on this waterlily have not come from the plant but from the water itself. They are bubbles of air which dissolved in the water overnight and then came out of solution, forming bubbles, as the water warmed.

Old Faithful, the ▶ famous geyser in Yellowstone Park, USA, takes about an hour to build up enough pressure to erupt.

In some parts of the world, the Earth's crust is so thin that water near to the surface is heated to boiling by the hot rocks underneath. This pool of boiling water has steam bubbles rising in its centre. ▶

Bubbles sometimes appear in water as if from nowhere. Clear water left standing in a glass may have lots of little bubbles in it after a few minutes. Air that was **dissolved** in the water has come out of **solution**, forming these bubbles. The bubbles form on the sides of the glass. Two things cause these bubbles. They form when the water is warmed, because warm water can hold less dissolved air than cold water. They also form when pressure is reduced. For instance, when you turn on a tap, the water that comes out is under less pressure than it was in the pipe—and so bubbles often form in fresh tap water.

The bubbles in boiling water are not air but **steam**. In some parts of the world, water is heated to boiling point by hot rocks deep underground and comes bursting to the surface as a **geyser**. Bubbles of steam in the underground water **expand** because the pressure falls as the water comes rushing upwards, causing it to squirt high into the air.

Bubbles out of Water

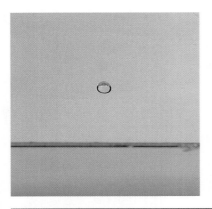
The petals of this Nasturtium have been shredded by large raindrops which came down with such force that they made bubbles on puddles as well.

Bubbles that rise in a pond or river usually burst when they get to the surface. Sometimes a bubble will float for a time and then you can see how it is formed from a thin layer of water. A large floating bubble is almost a **hemisphere**. Where its edge sits on the water, surface tension pulling inwards is exactly balanced by gas pressure pushing outwards, keeping the bubble in shape.

Soap or **detergent** added to water makes floating bubbles last longer. Some **polluted** rivers contain detergents, and that is why there are often masses of bubbles floating along on the surface.

▼ A large raindrop comes rushing down towards the surface of a pond.

▼ The raindrop smacks into the surface, sending up a circular sheet of water shaped like a crown.

▼ The force of the raindrop causes a round pit to form in the surface, while the crown-shaped sheet rises higher.

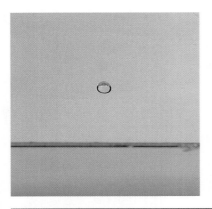

Animals such as worms and shrimps live in burrows on a muddy seashore. Their burrows become filled with air at low tide. When the tide comes in, this air is forced out, forming large floating bubbles.

◄

Detergents reduce surface tension. This means that the pulling force on the surface of bubbles is not so strong, and so they do not burst so easily. That is why it is possible to blow round bubbles that float in the air using water containing a little detergent (*see page 28*).

▼ Surface tension acts like a draw-string and begins to pull the top of the crown-shaped sheet inwards.

▼ The top of the crown is pulled together by the surface tension, forming a bubble, part of which is the pit in the water's surface.

▼ As the effect of the drop's force wears off, water at the bottom of the pit rushes upwards, forming a column which shoots up through the top of the bubble.

Breathing Bubbles

A Water Spider keeps a silvery-looking supply of air trapped amongst the hairs of its body so that it can breathe when it is under water. It also spins an underwater bell of silk. The spider brings air down to its **diving bell** until it is filled with a large bubble. This makes a safe place for the air-breathing spider to rest while it is waiting for prey. ▶

Water animals that breathe air have to keep coming to the surface. It can be dangerous for small creatures to do this often and so many carry a bubble of air with them. Some water beetles keep air under their **elytra**, or wing cases. Others have hairs on their undersides which hold a bubble of air, making them look silvery underneath. These beetles can stay under water for many minutes, or even hours, using their breathing bubbles. Other animals, such as newts and frogs, come to the surface to gulp air into their lungs before diving. They just hold their breath while they are under water.

Some animals that breathe water come onto land occasionally. They have to bring with them enough water to keep their **gills** wet. Crabs that come on to land take in some air to supply the water around their gills with oxygen. When they blow this air out, it often forms bubbles (*see pages 1 and 26*).

▲

A Great Diving Beetle is an air-breather. It takes a supply of air stored under its elytra when it dives. ▶

Whales and dolphins come to the surface regularly to take deep breaths so that they can store large amounts of oxygen in their blood and muscles. They breathe out again before they dive, but still take some air with them. Underwater, dolphins talk to each other in squeaks. When they squeak, a thin stream of bubbles sometimes comes out of the dolphin's **blowhole**.

Humpback Whales use streams of bubbles to round up fish. A group of whales swims around in a circle below a shoal of fish and each whale lets out a stream of bubbles. As the bubbles rise, they form a circular curtain through which the fish do not like to swim. Suddenly, the whales rush up from the depths and gulp down the fish!

Dolphins are air-breathing mammals. This one has just come to the surface of the sea to breathe. Its nostril, or blowhole, is wide open to take in air. ▲

Just before a dolphin surfaces, it empties its lungs of stale air. The air bursts out of its blowhole as a stream of bubbles. ▶

Humans cannot hold their breath for more than two or three minutes at the very most, and so divers have to take an air supply with them. A diver working in deep water breathes air at high pressure. The pressure causes **nitrogen** gas to dissolve in the diver's blood. When the diver comes up and the pressure is released, little bubbles of nitrogen may form in the blood, causing a painful—and sometimes fatal—condition called **diver's bends**. A whale does not suffer from the bends because it does not breathe while it is under water. It simply holds its breath for as long as half an hour.

Whales take several deep breaths before they dive. This makes sure that their blood is well supplied with oxygen while they are feeding underwater. At each breath, a cloud of spray and **condensation** rises into the air. Here, two whales are spouting close together. ▼

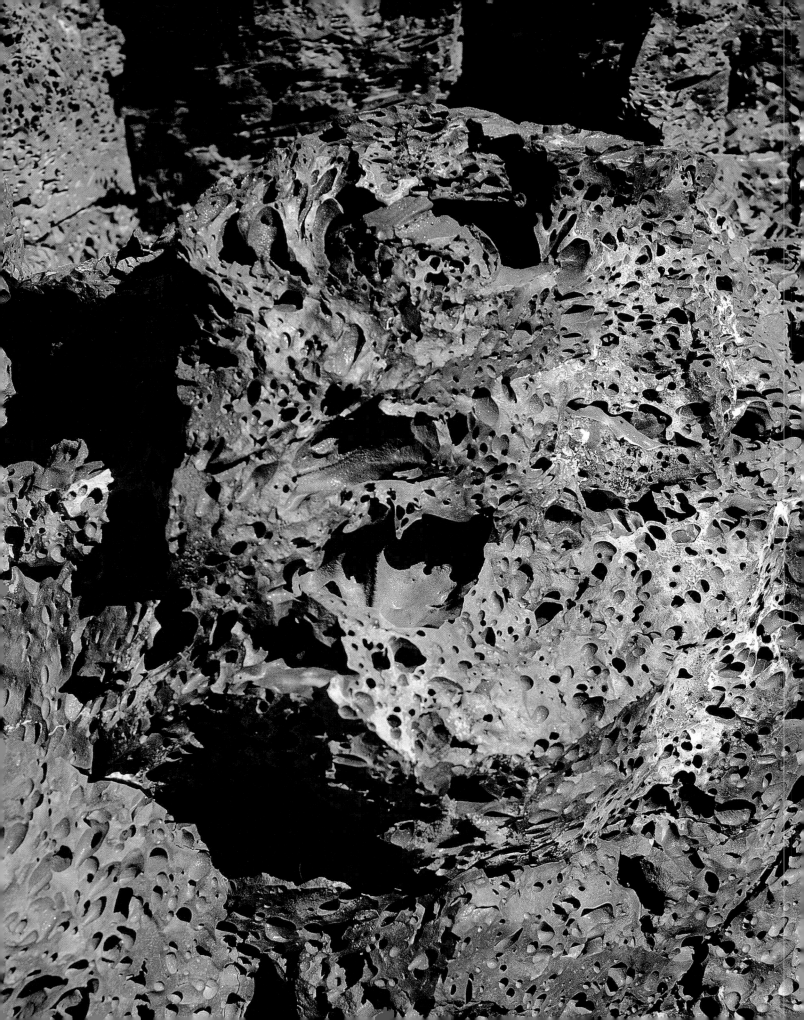

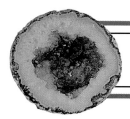

Frozen Bubbles

Bubbles can only form in a liquid. But liquids can **solidify**, trapping the bubbles. When violent volcanoes blow molten **lava** high into the air, the pressure is suddenly released and the lava becomes frothy and cools quickly. This frothy rock is called **pumice** and is so light that a chunk of it floats in water.

Bubbles that rise to the surface of a lake as it freezes are trapped beneath the ice. As the ice gets thicker, so the bubbles become encased in it. The ice sheets in Greenland and Antarctica are hundreds of metres thick and contain air bubbles that were trapped many thousands of years ago. By drilling deep holes in the ice and collecting the air from these bubbles, scientists can tell what the Earth's **atmosphere** was like all that time ago.

◀ A **geode** is a hollow ball, like a big bubble of gas set in rock. Inside, beautiful crystals of purple amethyst grow, pointing inwards.

Bubbles in a thick and sticky liquid rise only slowly to the surface. Red-hot molten lava is very thick and sticky, and gas bubbles often become trapped in it. The lava cools and sets into a rock full of holes.

Water is a clear liquid and it freezes into ice which is a clear solid. Yet **icebergs** look white, not clear. This is because most ice is filled with little bubbles. The bubbles **scatter** light passing through the ice, making it look white in sunlight, but blue on a dull day.

Bubble Wrap

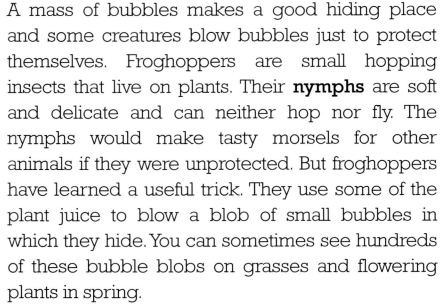

This male Siamese Fighting Fish is at the surface taking in a bubble of air. He makes a floating nest for his eggs by spitting out mucus-coated bubbles.

A mass of bubbles makes a good hiding place and some creatures blow bubbles just to protect themselves. Froghoppers are small hopping insects that live on plants. Their **nymphs** are soft and delicate and can neither hop nor fly. The nymphs would make tasty morsels for other animals if they were unprotected. But froghoppers have learned a useful trick. They use some of the plant juice to blow a blob of small bubbles in which they hide. You can sometimes see hundreds of these bubble blobs on grasses and flowering plants in spring.

There are other animals that also wrap their eggs or young in bubbles to protect them. Some species of tree frog lay their eggs on twigs above ponds. They produce slime when they are egg-laying and kick their hind legs in it to make bubbles. The eggs are then hanging in a ball of sticky white **froth**. The **tadpoles** hatch into the froth and swim around in it for a while before dropping into the pond below.

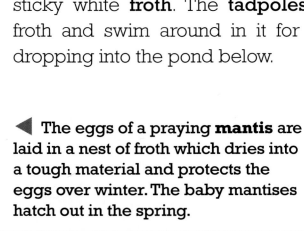

◀ The eggs of a praying **mantis** are laid in a nest of froth which dries into a tough material and protects the eggs over winter. The baby mantises hatch out in the spring.

A froghopper nymph feeds on plant **sap** using its **proboscis** to pierce the stem of the plant. It draws more sap than it needs for food and uses some of it to form a mass of bubbles in which it hides from its enemies.

Bubbles Make Floats

Egg or Knotted Wrack needs large **bladders** to buoy up its thick, rubbery **fronds**. ▲

Many water animals use bubbles as floats, either to keep themselves on the surface or so that they can hang in mid-water without sinking. Phantom Midge **larvae** have a pair of bubbles at each end so that their bodies hang level in the water. Violet Sea Snails use slime to blow a small collection of tough bubbles which keep them floating on the surface of the sea. Another sea creature called a Portuguese Man-of-war has a clear bubble-like float. When the wind blows, Portuguese Men-of-war go scudding over the ocean with their **tentacles** trailing in the water below.

Portuguese Men-of-war are related to jellyfish. They have transparent bladders that float on the surface. These Men-of-war have been washed up on the shore among some seaweed. ▶

The fronds of Bladder Wrack contain many gas-filled bladders. These support the plant in the water so that, when the tide comes in, the fronds float upright instead of lying on the bottom.

Strictly speaking, the Man-of-war's float is not a bubble because it is not formed of a liquid. It is a bladder. A bladder consists of a thin layer of elastic material. A rubber balloon is a good example of a bladder. Some seaweeds, such as Bladder Wrack, collect oxygen in bladders so that their fronds float up over the rocky seabed when the tide comes in.

Phantom Midge larvae have nearly transparent bodies and hang motionless in fresh water pools, waiting for prey. Their bodies are supported by two pairs of air bubbles, one near the head and one near the tail.

Being able to hang in mid-water is useful if you are a fish. You can have a rest without fear of sinking to the bottom. Most fishes can control their position in the water so that they neither float nor sink. They do this by using a tough bag inside their bodies called a **swim bladder**. A fish's swim bladder contains a bubble of oxygen. Oxygen dissolved in the blood is used to control the size of the bubble in the swim bladder, which adjusts the fish's position in the water.

Gases can be **compressed**. The floating power of a bubble is related to its size, not the amount of gas in it. Squeeze a big bubble (or bladder) into a smaller space, and it will not float so strongly. When a fish dives into deeper water, its swim bladder is squeezed smaller. The fish then has to pump more oxygen into it in order to stop itself from sinking even deeper.

These African lake fishes can rise or sink or remain motionless in the water simply by adjusting the amount of oxygen in their swim bladders.
◀

A pair of Common Frogs float at the surface, breathing air.
▼

When the frogs dive, they expel some air bubbles so that it is easier for them to swim to the bottom of the pond.
▼

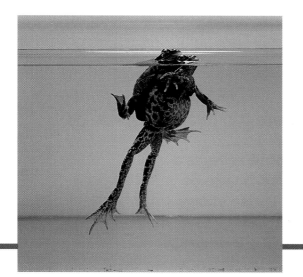

 # Looking into Bubbles

The bubbles floating on this stream make lenses through which you can see reduced images of the plants and gravel below. If you look very carefully, you may see images of a little yellow fish in some of the bubbles. Wobbly, but life-size, images appear in the pattern of **concentric** rings left by a bubble that has just burst. ▶

Bubbles in water often look silvery. This is because an underwater bubble is a kind of **lens**. If you look through a bubble which has formed on the side of a glass of water, you can see in it a greatly reduced **image** of what is beyond. The image is very **distorted** but, if you hold the glass up to the window, you might be able to make out a whole house across the street with the sky above it. It is the image of the sky that makes the top of the bubble look silvery.

Floating bubbles and soap bubbles in air are not lenses. They act as curved mirrors, reflecting a distorted image of things around them. However the most fascinating thing about soap bubbles is their colours. These colours depend on the thickness of the water film making the bubble. A freshly formed bubble is thick and has no colours. As the bubble is blown bigger, its wall stretches and becomes thinner. Green and red colours appear. The wall of a free bubble continues to get thinner because water **evaporates** from it, and it becomes yellow, blue and purple before it bursts (*see page 28*).

◀ A floating bubble reflects a very much reduced image of its surroundings. It also shows rainbow colours.

Bubble Baths

A fiddler crab takes ▲ in air to supply the water around its gills with oxygen. When it blows the air out, some of the water comes out as well, forming bubbles.

Wherever there is water, you will almost always find bubbles. Even in a still pool there are often strings of tiny bubbles rising from the bottom. A rushing river with waterfalls is full of bubbles and, in places, the water looks white because of all the bubbles in it. Waves in a rough sea also make masses of bubbles. Sometimes these form froth on the surface which the wind then picks up and carries inland.

Bubbles are a fascinating result of liquid and gas coming together, and surface tension is the vital force that allows them to form. It tries to make all bubbles round. But bubbles can be pulled or pushed out of shape or broken into smaller bubbles by other forces.

Breaking waves ▶ cause pure white foam to form in clean sea water. The bubbles making up the foam may only last a few seconds before they burst. This is because the surface tension of sea water is fairly high. These Grey Seals are coming ashore through the breakers.

Some water animals carry with them their own bubble of air for breathing while some land animals hide in frothy balls of bubbles. Fish use gas bubbles in their swim bladders to regulate their depth in the water. But people use bubbles mostly just for baths and for fun!

A huge waterfall, ▲ like Niagara, makes plenty of foam but the foam does not last for long. The bubbles soon burst as they are carried downstream.

Things to Do:
Playing with Bubbles

Bubble Colours

The colours in a soap bubble seem quite magical. Water has no colour. The soap or detergent you add to water to make the bubbles may give the mixture only a faint green or yellow tinge yet, when a bubble is blown, it shows the purest rainbow colours. Where do these colours come from? The answer lies in the nature of light itself.

To study the colours in bubbles, you need a plastic beaker and a small disposable plastic container—a film canister is ideal. Punch several holes in the bottom of the canister with a skewer.

The wall of this bubble is thin at the top, but gets thicker towards the bottom, causing bands of colour.

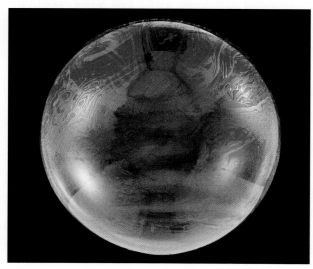

(Ask an adult to help you do this.) Half fill the beaker with water and add a small squirt of washing-up liquid. Mix well and you are now ready to blow bubbles. Dip the open end of the canister in the mixture briefly and then blow through the holes you have made in it. Note how, when the bubble starts to form, it has no colour. As you continue blowing, reds and greens appear. At this stage you can try freeing the bubble by moving the canister quickly sideways.

The longer you can keep the bubble "alive", the more interesting its colours will become. Probably the best way of doing this is to choose a cold windless day and to blow your bubbles outdoors. A cold day is better than a warm one because your warm breath inside the bubbles will cause them to rise in cold air. They may even go sailing over the rooftops!

A red and green bubble hanging in the air on a bright, cold morning is a wonderful sight. Gradually its colour changes to gold, then blue and purple. Finally, it may go completely colourless again or holes may seem to appear in it shortly before it bursts. The reason for these colour changes is that water is constantly evaporating from the bubble, causing its wall to get thinner. And it is the thinness of the bubble's wall that determines its colour.

Light from the sun is made up of all the colours of the rainbow mixed together and each colour has a slightly different **wavelength**. When the thickness of the bubble's wall matches the wavelength of a particular colour, that colour is reflected by the bubble instead of passing straight through it, and so you see that colour. You can understand that the waves of light are very close together indeed—no further apart than the thickness of a bubble's wall, which is a minute fraction of a millimetre. So, as water evaporates and the bubble's wall thins, the longest wavelength light (red) is reflected first and the shortest wavelength (purple) last. When holes seem to appear in the bubble or it stops reflecting altogether, the wall has become so thin that all light visible to us passes straight through. Only ultraviolet light is reflected. We cannot see ultraviolet but some insects and birds can.

Negative Bubbles

A soap bubble is a thin film of water floating about in air. Might it be possible to have the opposite—a thin film of air floating about in water? The idea does not seem very likely. How would you blow such a bubble for a start? Well, **negative bubbles**, as they are called, do exist and they are quite easy to make, although they never get very big. All you need is a clear glass or plastic container in which to form the negative bubbles, a spoon, a small jug and some liquid detergent. Fill the container to near the top with water and add a little detergent. Fill the jug with ''detergenty'' water by dipping it into the container. Hold the spoon the right way up just above the surface of the water in the container and gently pour water into it from the jug (above right). Vary the height of the spoon above the water and the flow from the jug until silvery beads of water start to skate over the surface. Eventually,

A negative bubble is formed of a thin film of air in water. It is not filled with air, but instead contains a blob of water.

some of these beads will get pushed beneath the surface taking a film of air with them and forming the mysterious and elusive negative bubbles. They drift only slowly towards the surface and look different from normal underwater bubbles because, like soap bubbles in air, they do not form lenses.

When a negative bubble bursts, a few small air bubbles race upwards towards the surface. This is just the opposite to what happens when a soap bubble bursts in the air. Then, a few small drops of water race downwards towards the ground.

An air bubble, trapped in the clear jelly of frog spawn, works as a lens, producing small images of the growing tadpoles.

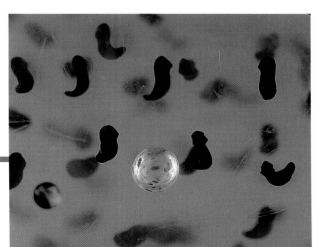

Glossary

Air: The mixture of gases, mostly oxygen and nitrogen, that surrounds the Earth.
Atmosphere: The layer of air and clouds that surrounds the Earth.

Bladder: A bag that can be filled with gas or liquid.
Blowhole: A hole on the top of the head of whales, dolphins and porpoises through which they breathe.

Compress: To squeeze into a smaller space.
Concentric: Having the same centre.
Condensation: Water that has come out of the air as droplets.

Detergent: A cleaning material which helps oil and water to mix. Washing up liquid is a detergent.
Dissolved: Mixed completely with a liquid. Sugar dissolves in water but sand does not.
Distort: To twist something out of shape.
Diver's bends: A dangerous and painful condition experienced by divers who come to the surface too quickly.
Diving bell: A heavy bell-shaped chamber in which men were lowered into the sea during the early days of underwater exploration. Modern forms are still used by underwater workers.

Elastic: Able to recover its original shape after being stretched.
Elytra: The hardened forewings under which beetles keep their folded hind wings. Singular: elytrum.
Evaporate: To change from liquid to vapour.

Expand: To get larger or occupy more space.

Film: A very thin layer.

Frond: A long leaf or leaf-like structure.
Froth: Masses of small bubbles sticking together.

Geode: A hollow ball of rock often containing crystals on the inner surface
Genus: The name given to a group of similar species. Plural: genera. The Large White Butterfly *(Pieris brassicae)* and the Small White Butterfly *(Pieris rapae)* are separate species in the same genus.
Geyser: A jet of hot water and steam coming out of the ground.
Gills: The organs used by water animals for breathing.

Hemisphere: Half of a round, ball-shaped object or sphere.

Iceberg: A huge block of ice broken off a glacier or ice shelf and floating in the sea.
Image: A picture

Lava: Molten rock spewed out by volcanoes.
Larvae: The early stages in the growth of some animals. Singular: larva.
Lens: A piece of clear material with curved sides that will focus light.

Mantis: A type of insect with strong front legs for catching prey.
Methane: A gas made from carbon and hydrogen. Chemical formula: CH_4.

Negative bubble: A bubble formed of a thin film of air in water.

Nitrogen: A gas forming nearly four fifths of the air. Chemical symbol: N.
Nymph: The young and normally wingless stages of many kinds of insects.

Oxygen: A gas, essential for life, forming about one fifth of the air. Chemical symbol: O.

Polluted: Containing waste chemicals and rubbish.
Pressure: A force that squeezes or compresses.
Proboscis: The tube-like mouth parts of some insects.
Pumice: A kind of rock full of bubbles formed when molten, frothy lava is cooled quickly.

Sap: The liquid found inside plants.
Scatter: To send off or bounce in all directions.
Solidify: To turn from liquid into solid.
Solution: A liquid that contains a dissolved solid or gas.
Species: A biologically distinct kind of animal or plant. Similar species are grouped into the same genus. The word species can be singular or plural.
Steam: Water that has been turned into gas by heat. Water normally turns to steam at 100 degrees Centigrade.
Surface tension: The layer at the surface of a liquid which acts like a stretched, elastic skin.
Swim bladder: A gas-filled bladder inside fishes which they use to control their depth in the water.

Tadpole: The larva of frogs, toads, newts, salamanders etc.
Tentacles: Thin wavy arms used by some animals for grasping or gathering food.

Wavelength: The distance between waves.

Plants and Animals

The *common names* of plants and animals vary from place to place. Their *scientific names*, based on Greek or Latin words, are the same the world over. Each kind of plant or animal has two scientific names—like a first name and a surname for a person—except that the names are placed the other way round. The name of the **genus**, or *generic name*, which is like a surname, always comes first and starts with a capital letter. The name of the **species**, or *specific name*, comes second and always begins with a small letter. In this book, capitals are used for the initial letters of common names to make it clear when a particular species is being referred to.

Goldfish *(Carassius auratus)*—domesticated, kept worldwide **Cover**

Red Waterlily *(Nymphaea)*—cultivated worldwide **Cover, 8**

Rock Crab *(Leptograpsus variegatus)*—West and South West Australia **1**

Green seaweed *(Caulerpa)*—tropical seas **4**

Blue Gourami *(Trichogaster trichopterus)*—South East Asia **5**

Pearl Gourami *(Trichogaster leeri)*—South East Asia **5**

Avocet *(Recurvirostra avosetta)*—Europe, Africa **7**

Butterfly Fish *(Pantodon bulchholzi)*—West Africa **8**

Nasturtium *(Tropaeolum majus)*—South America, cultivated worldwide **10**

Great Diving Beetle *(Dytiscus marginalis)*—Europe **12, 31**

Water Spider *(Argyroneta aquatica)*—Europe **13**

Common Dolphin *(Delphinus delphis)*—seas worldwide **14**

Blue Whale *(Balaenoptera musculus)*—Atlantic and Pacific Oceans **15**

Adelie Penguin *(Pygoscelis adeliae)*—Antarctica **17**

Siamese Fighting Fish *(Betta splendens)*—Malay Peninsula and Thailand **18**

Large Mantis *(Paratenodera ardifolia)*—Japan **18**

Froghopper *(Philaenus spumarius)*—Europe **19**

Egg or Knotted Wrack *(Aescophyllum nodosum)*—North Atlantic shores **20**

Bladder Wrack *(Fucus vesiculosus)*—North Atlantic shores **20**

Portuguese Man-of-war *(Physalia)*—warm oceans **21**

Phantom Midge *(Chaoborus crystallinus)*—Europe **21**

Yellow Cichlid *(Neolamprologus leleupi)*—East Africa **22**

Blue-banded Cichlid *(Neolamprologus tretocephalus)*—East Africa (Other fishes not identified) **22**

Common Frog *(Rana temporaria)*—Europe **23, 29**

Lemon Tetra *(Hyphessobrycon pulchripinnis)*—South America **25**

Amazon Sword Plant *(Echinodorus paniculatus)*—South America **25**

Fanwort *(Cabomba aquatica)*—South America **25**

Fiddler Crab *(Uca)*—North and South America **26**

Grey Seal *(Halochoerus grypus)*—North Atlantic Coasts **26**

Index